Kia ora, e hoa mā

Welcome to this little book about the Māori way of life.

Tikanga Māori includes Māori customs, practices and ways of doing things. As you grow up in Aotearoa, you and your whānau can experience many principles of tikanga Māori in action. This pukapuka will tell you about some of them and the special words we use to talk about tikanga.

You may come across different tikanga throughout Aotearoa, which is part of what makes each iwi unique. We can enjoy these experiences if we follow four words that all start with 'wh': whakarongo (listen), whanonga (behaviour, behave with respect), whakawhetai (give thanks), whakaiti (be humble, open to learning). If you have this book, you are open to learning already. I think that's a wonderful start.

Ahakoa he iti, he pounamu — although it is small, it is precious.

May these small words be precious to your whānau.

Stacey

E whakamiha atu nei ki ngā Pouako, ngā Pou tikanga i tā koutou manaaki mai. With huge gratitude and respect for the teachers and tikanga experts who look after us.
— Stacey

He ngākaunui tēnei ki te hunga nā rātou ngā pūkenga, pūmanawa me ngā mōhiotanga ki ngā tikanga. Ko te manako ia, he puka whakaohooho tēnei i te reanga ringatoi e heke mai ana. Dedicated to all those that have contributed their talent, artistry and knowledge of tikanga. We hope this book will inspire future generations of artists to come.
— Tīma Kurawaka

PUFFIN
First published by Penguin Random House New Zealand, 2023
10 9 8 7 6 5 4 3 2 1

Design by Katrina Duncan © Penguin Random House New Zealand,
based on *My First Words in Māori* series design by Ali Teo and John O'Reilly
Photograph of Stacey Morrison courtesy of the Breast Cancer Foundation NZ
Illustration of Kurawaka team by Kurawaka Animation Productions
'Tūtira Mai Ngā Iwi' waiata composed by Wiremu Te Tau Huata (Ngāti Kahungunu)
Printed and bound in China by RR Donnelley
Produced using vegetable-based inks
A catalogue record for this book is available from the National Library of New Zealand.
ISBN 978-1-77695-706-4
The assistance of Creative New Zealand towards the production
of this book is gratefully acknowledged by the publisher.

penguin.co.nz

My First Words about Tikanga Māori

Stacey Morrison

illustrations by
Kurawaka Productions

PUFFIN

Karakia

Words of power

Me karakia tātou.
Let's all say karakia together.

Tūtawa mai i runga
From above

Tūtawa mai i raro
From below

Tūtawa mai i roto
From within

Tūtawa mai i waho
From all around us

Kia tau ai te mauri tū,
te mauri ora ki te katoa
We call for positive energy
for everybody here

Haumi e, hui e, tāiki e!
Bringing us all together!

Wairua
Spirit

Tinana
Body

Hui
Meeting, event

Karakia call on good energy for our minds, our hinengaro, and our wairua, our spirit. That's why you will hear karakia to begin and finish hui.

Tīmatanga
Beginning

Whakakapi
To finish

Pōwhiri
Formal welcome

Kaikaranga
The person who performs karanga

Kaikōrero
The person who performs whaikōrero

Tangata whenua
Home people, hosts

This is what a pōwhiri at school could look like.

Kaumātua
Elderly people

Manuhiri
Guests

Ope
Group of people moving together

Karanga
Calls of welcome and reply

Whaikōrero
Formal speech

Harirū
Shaking hands, greeting each other with hongi

Tikanga Māori gives us a special way to welcome people to occasions such as hui or events.

Nau mai, haere mai e te iwi e!
Come in, welcome to you all!

Tihei mauri ora!
Behold the breath of life!

Whare
Meeting house

Koha
Donation

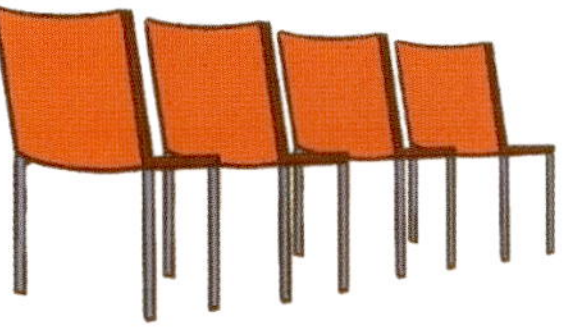

Paepae
Seats in the first row, for kaikōrero

Haka pōwhiri
Haka of welcome

Tokotoko
Carved walking stick

Hongi
Our unique greeting

Once the manuhiri have been welcomed by the tangata whenua we line up to shake hands and hongi.

In this unique Māori greeting, we recognise the mauri — the lifeforce — of the other person.

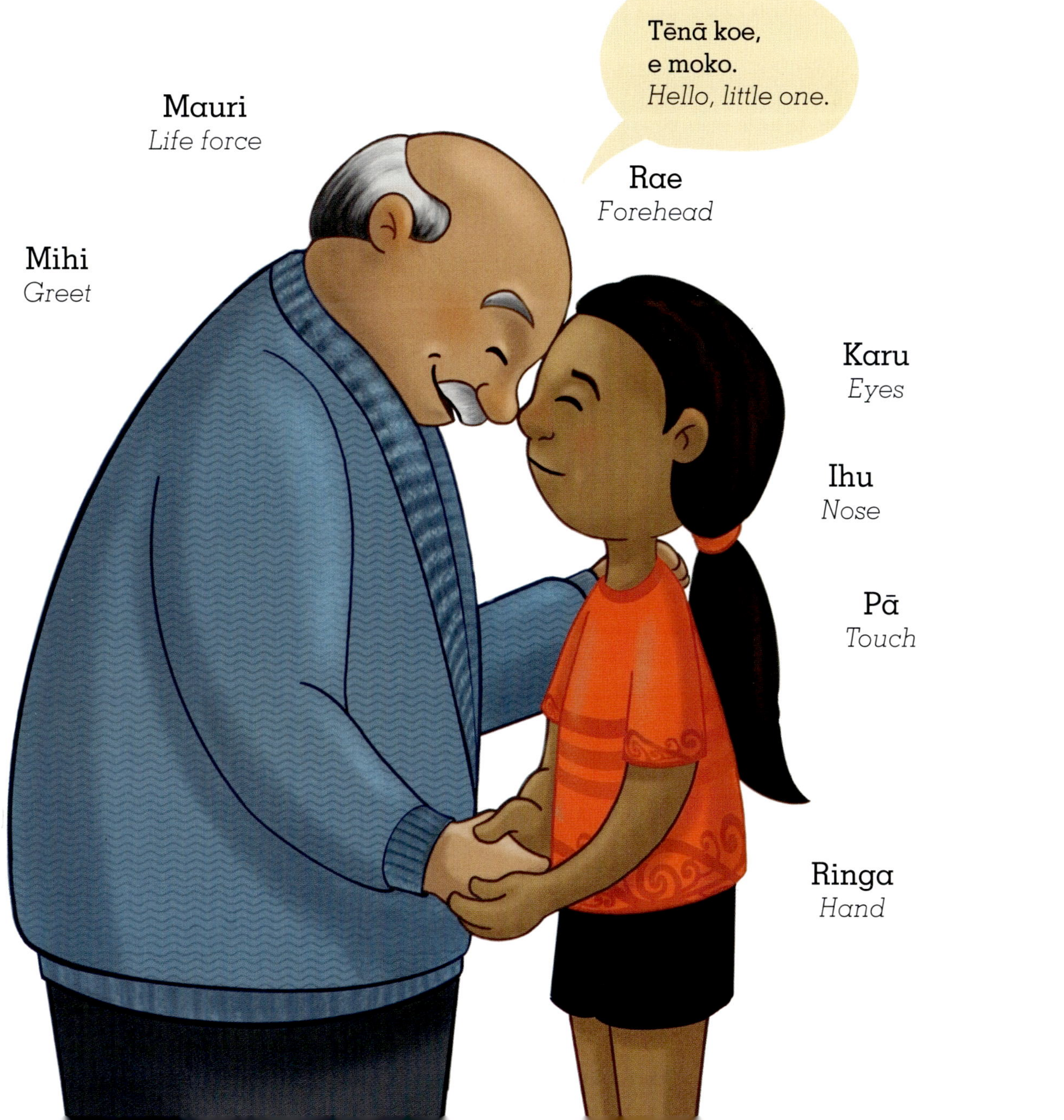

Tēnā koe, e moko.
Hello, little one.

Mauri
Life force

Rae
Forehead

Mihi
Greet

Karu
Eyes

Ihu
Nose

Pā
Touch

Ringa
Hand

Waiata
Songs, singing

Waiata
Song, singing

Kaiwaiata
Singer

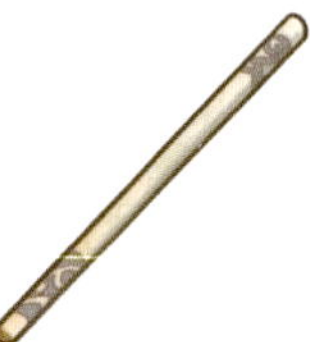

Tī rākau
Wooden sticks used in some waiata

Me waiata tahi tātou!
Let's all sing together!

Rakuraku
Guitar

Kaiako
Teacher

Kaea
Leader

Kaihaka
Haka performers

Kākahu
Clothes, cloak

Piupiu
Flax skirt

Singing waiata together is fun and also lifts our energy after karakia or whaikōrero.

Toru, whā — timata!
Three, four — start!

Tūtira mai ngā iwi, auē!
Stand together, people!

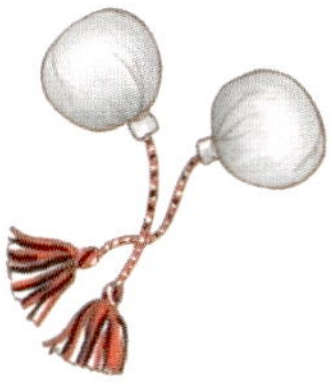

Poi
A light ball on a plaited length of wool

Kapa haka
Haka performing group

Rōpū
Group

Hui, mihimihi

Meetings and greetings

There are many types of hui you might go to.

Poukai

Hui for Kīngitanga

Hui ā-iwi

Iwi meetings

Noho marae

Marae stay

Tangihanga/Tangi

Māori funeral

Hura kōhatu

Unveiling

Mokopapa wānanga

Wānanga where a group of people receive moko

Wānanga

Hui for learning and discussion

At almost every hui there will be mihimihi, when everyone introduces themselves so they can get to know each other.

Tēnā koutou, ko ________________ tōku ingoa.
Hello to you all. My name is ___________.

Nō ______________ ahau.
I am from . . . (e.g. Aotearoa, place where you come from, or your iwi)

Kia ora!

Whakataetae
Competition

Whakataetae ā-rohe
Regional competitions

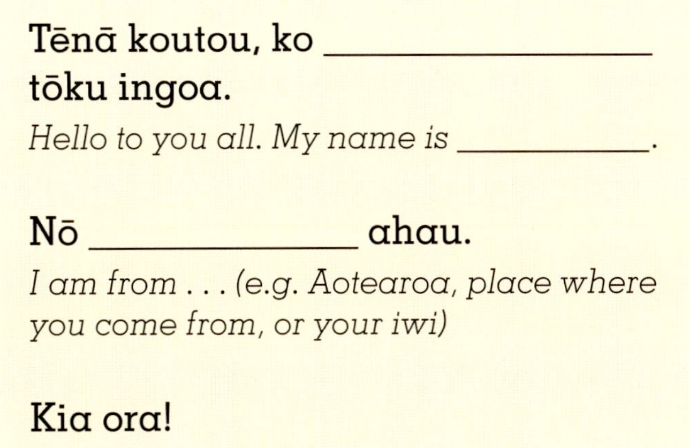

Whakangahau
Concert, entertainment

Whakataetae kapa haka
Kapa haka competitions

Te Matatini
National kapa haka competitions

Whakatau
A welcome less formal than a pōwhiri

Kōrero ki ngā pakeke

Talking to adults

Even if adults aren't our actual parent, aunty, uncle or grandparent, we use these names to show respect and friendliness.

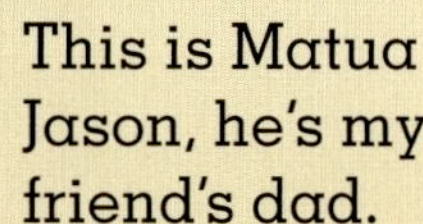

Pirimia
Prime Minister

Whaea
Mum, Aunty, woman

Matua
Dad, Uncle, man

Tumuaki
Principal

Rangatira
Chief, boss

Minita
Minister

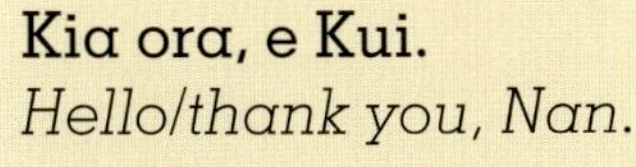

Kui
Grandmother, elderly woman

Koro
Grandfather, elderly man

Whakarākei

Adornments

Our Māori styles of dress are inspired by the traditions and creativity of our ancestors.

Have you seen Māori wearing or carrying these things?

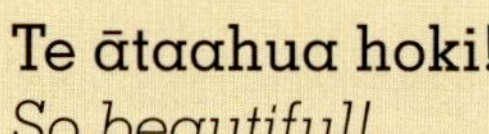

Te ātaahua hoki!
So beautiful!

Whakakai
Earrings

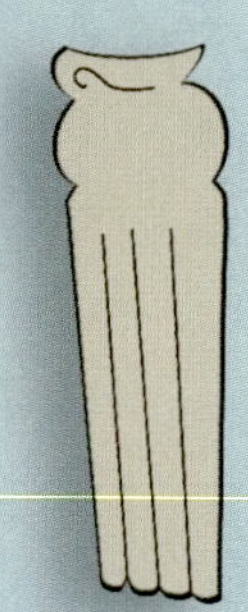

Heru
Comb

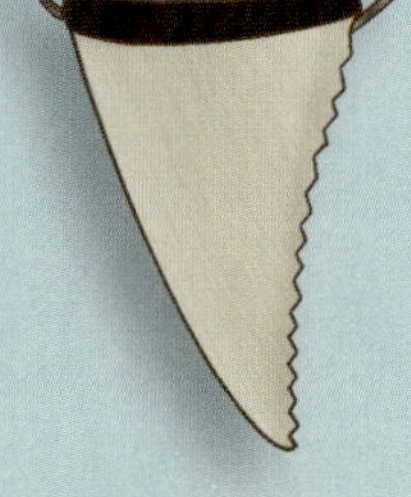

Niho mako
Shark tooth

Taonga
Treasure

Hei
Necklace

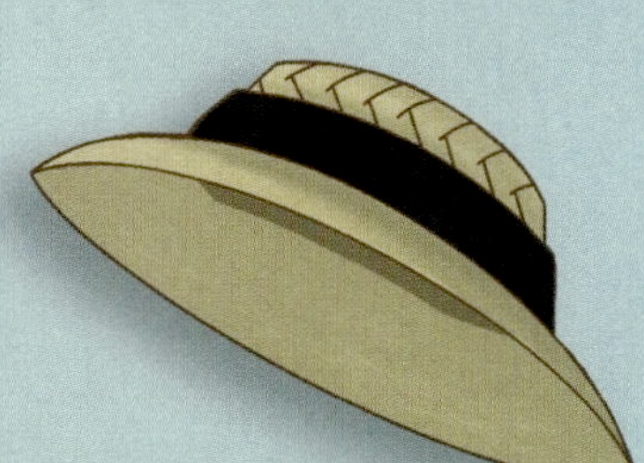

Pōtae
Hat

Kākahu
Clothing, some cloaks
Korowai
Cloak with tassels
Raukura
Feather plume
Kete
Basket or purse
Pīkau
Backpack kete
Taiaha
Long wooden staff
Patu
Club
Pūtātara
Conch shell trumpet

Te taiao

The environment

When we talk about the elements of the natural world we think of them as atua, powerful ancestors.

Huarere
Weather

Ua
Rain

Kapua
Clouds

Uira
Lightning

Hinetakurua
Atua of winter

Ruaumoko
Atua of earthquakes

Tāwhirimātea
Atua of the wind and weather

Papatūānuku
Earth Mother

Our maunga are special places; they are ancestors to us.

Maunga
Mountain

Puke
Hill

Tātahi
Beach

Nau mai, Tamanuiterā!
Here comes the sun!

Ranginui
Sky Father

Tamanuiterā
Atua of the sun

Moana
Sea

Awa
River

Tangaroa
Atua of the sea

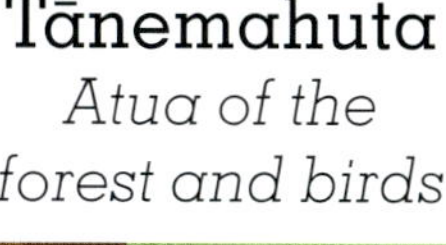

Tānemahuta
Atua of the forest and birds

Roto
Lake

Hineraumati
Atua of summer

Tēnā koe, Pōua Aoraki!
Hello there, grandfather Aoraki!

Whenua
Land

Ngahere
Forest

Whakaaro Māori

Māori concepts

Māori ways of looking at the world guide our actions and remind us of our special bonds.

Aroha
Love, compassion, caring

Manaaki
Hospitality

Whanaungatanga
Close relationships, looking after each other

Kaitiakitanga
Being a guardian for the environment

Mana
Authority, power, charisma and uniqueness

Tapu
Sacred, under restrictions so that people and places are protected physically and spiritually

Noa
To be free from tapu

Rāhui
A temporary ban on using something so it can recover, or until tapu is removed

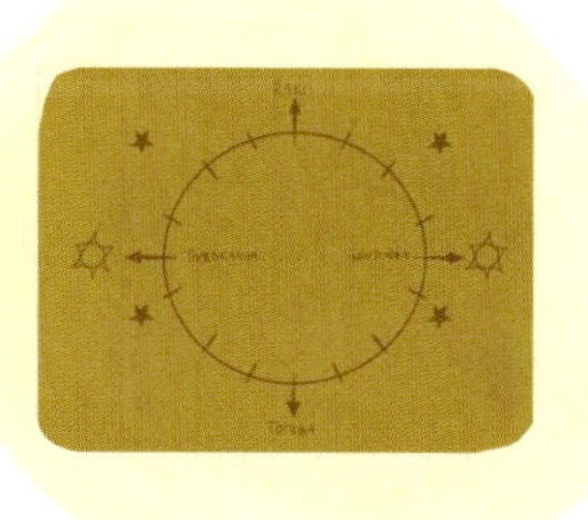

Mātauranga Māori
Māori knowledge and worldview

Kotahitanga
Unity, belonging

Pā, marae, papa kāinga

Māori communities

Papa kāinga
Communal home for hapū, iwi

Nau mai, haere mai ki tō tātou marae!
Welcome to our marae!

Pā
Village

Wharenui
Meeting house

Marae ātea
Front courtyard

Tangohia ō hū.
Take off your shoes.

Mahau
Porch (of meeting house)

Waharoa
Entrance to a pā

Kāuta/Kīhini
Kitchen

These are places where we live, gather, share food, and connect with each other as a community. When we say 'marae', we refer to the whole area of the wharenui, wharekai and marae ātea.

Kei hea a Māmā?
Where's Mum?

Wharekai
Dining room

Iwi
Tribe

Hapū
Sub tribe

Kei te pā ia.
She's at the pā.

Māra kai
Vegetable gardens

Pātaka
Storehouse raised on posts

Matariki, Puanga and Puaka

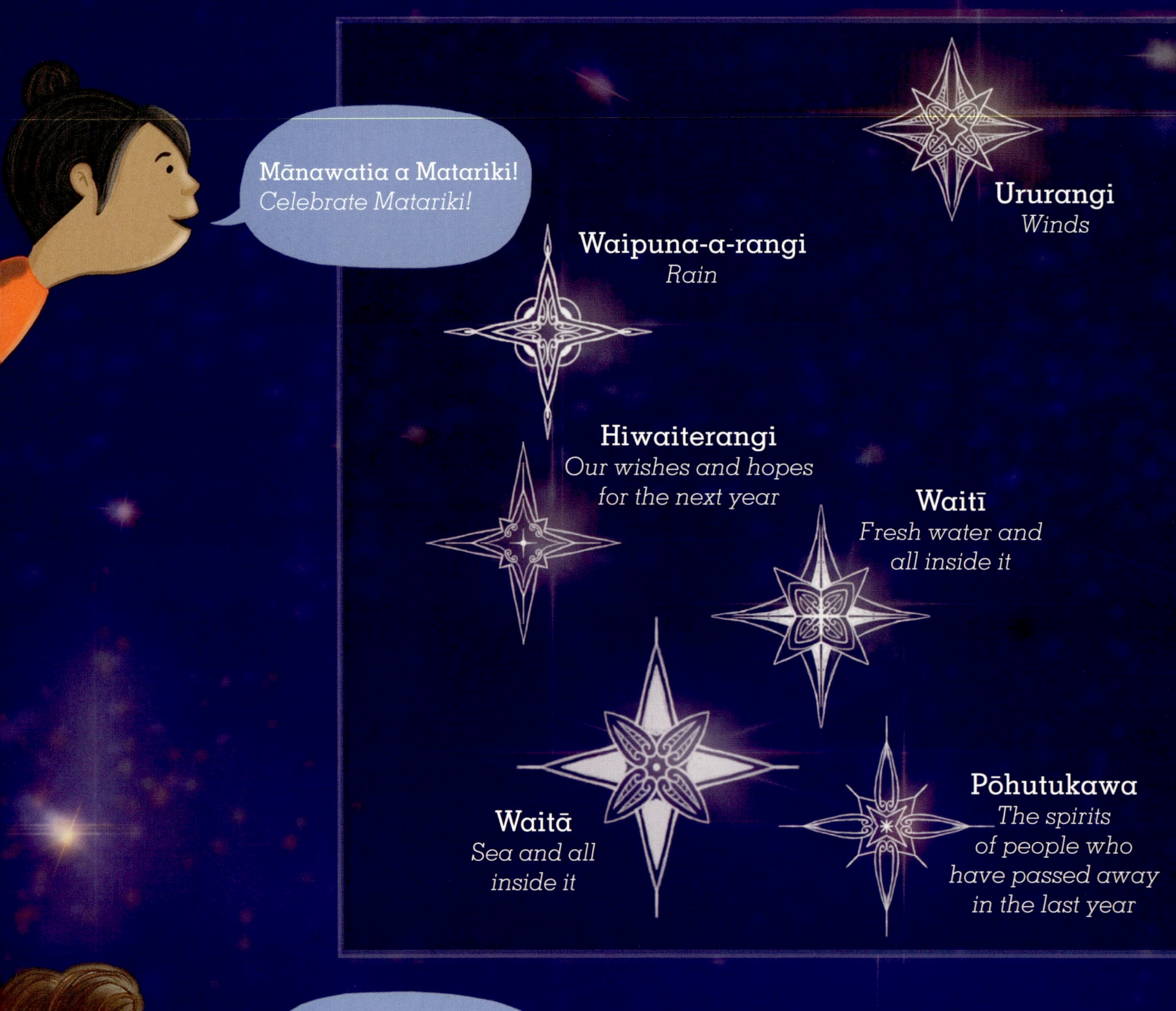

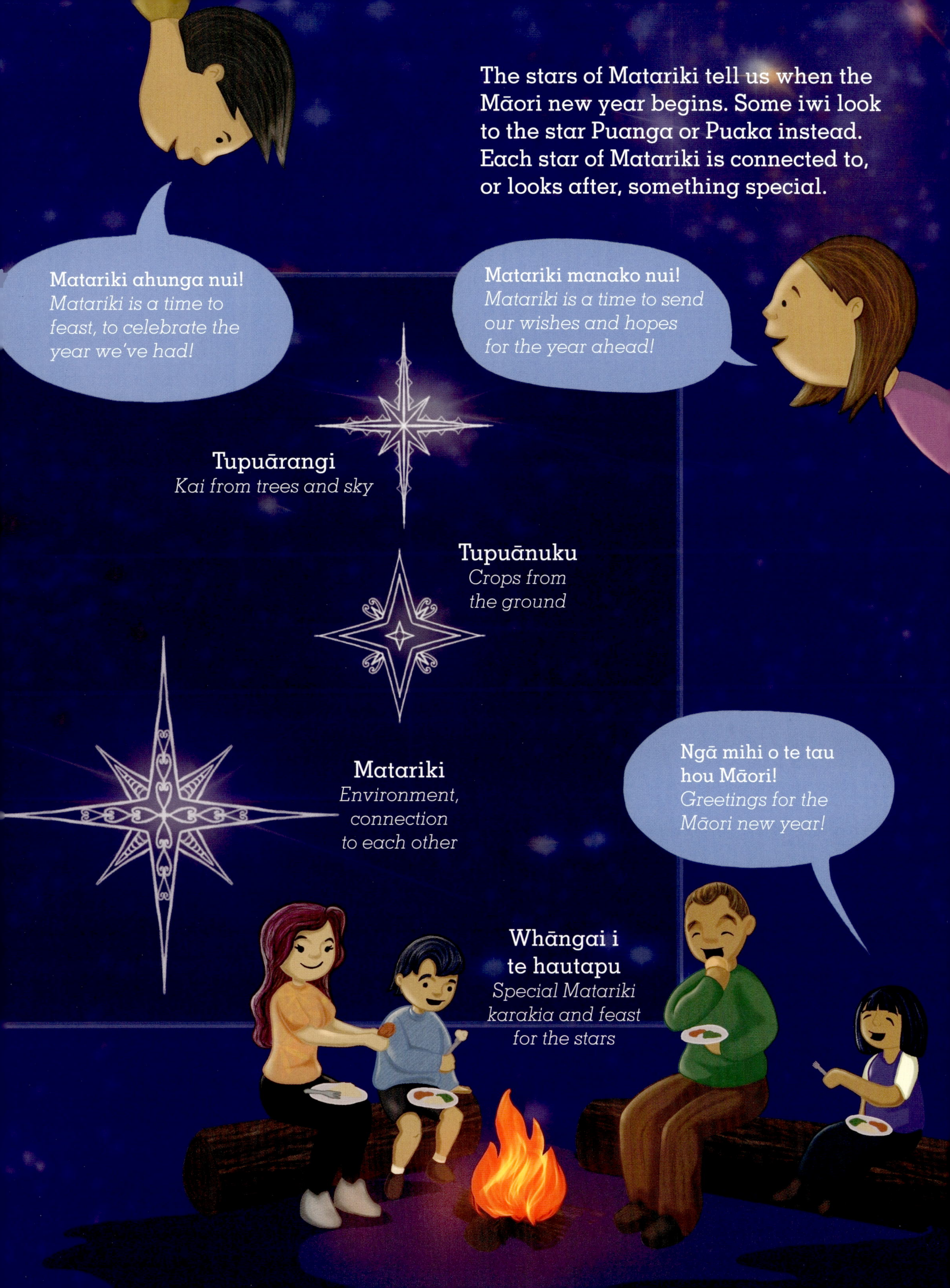
The stars of Matariki tell us when the Māori new year begins. Some iwi look to the star Puanga or Puaka instead. Each star of Matariki is connected to, or looks after, something special.
Matariki ahunga nui!
Matariki is a time to feast, to celebrate the year we've had!
Matariki manako nui!
Matariki is a time to send our wishes and hopes for the year ahead!
Tupuārangi
Kai from trees and sky
Tupuānuku
Crops from the ground
Matariki
Environment, connection to each other
Ngā mihi o te tau hou Māori!
Greetings for the Māori new year!
Whāngai i te hautapu
Special Matariki karakia and feast for the stars

Kai Māori

Māori foods

Eating together is another part of our tikanga of manaakitanga — hospitality. Feeding visitors well helps them feel welcome.

Ipu
Bowl, container

Pereti
Plate

Huarākau
Fruit

Huawhenua
Vegetables

Towhiro/Purini
Dessert

Haere mai ki te kai!
Come to eat!

Kai
Food

How many of these kai Māori have you tried?

Kānga pirau
Rotten corn

Hākari
Feast

Rēwena
Māori bread

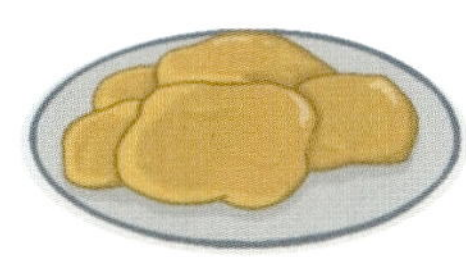

Parāoa parai
Fry bread

Kōura
Crayfish

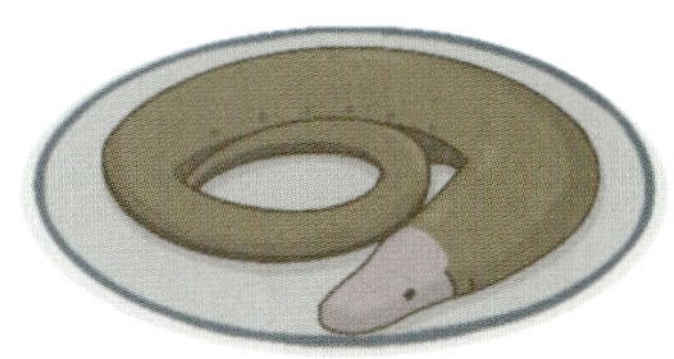

Tuna
Eel

Ringawera
Workers in the kitchen

Inu
Drink

Kaua e noho ki te tēpu kai.
Don't sit on the kai table.

Horoi rīhi
Dish-washing

Kapu
Cup

He reka te kai!
This food is delicious!

Kaimoana
Seafood

Pāua
Pāua/sea abalone, often creamed

Kūtai
Mussels

Tītī
Muttonbird

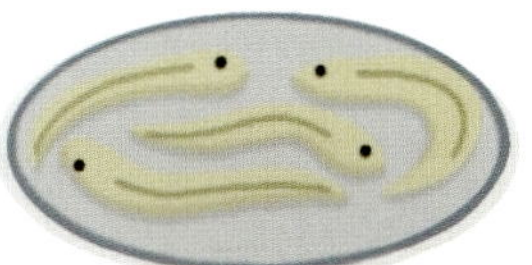

Inanga
Whitebait

Kina
Sea urchins

Hāngi/Umu
Kai cooked in the ground, or hāngi cooker

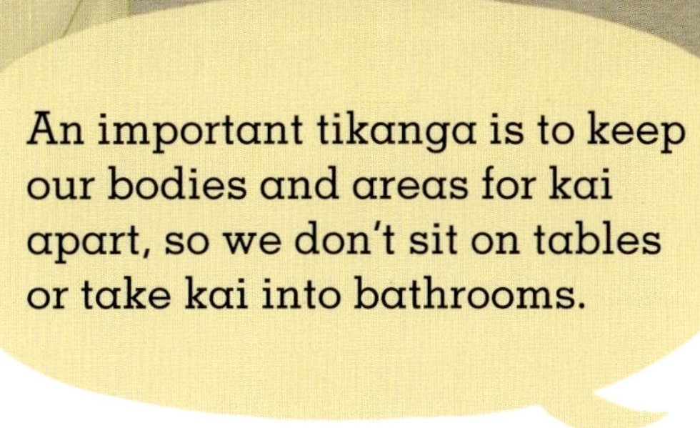

Tikanga o te kāinga

Tikanga at home

Tangohia ō hū
Take your shoes off

Waiho ō mōhiti me tō pōtae ki tētahi tūru
Leave your glasses and hat on a seat (not a place where kai goes)

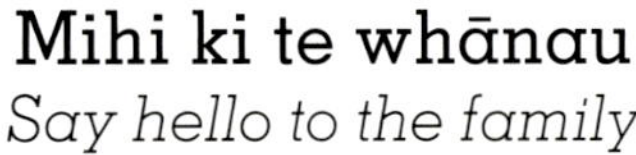

Mihi ki te whānau
Say hello to the family

Tēnā koe, Matua.
Hello, Uncle.

Karakia kai
Give thanks for the food we're about to enjoy

Nau mai, e ngā hua o Papaahurewa,
Ranginui kete kai, whītiki kia ora,
haumi e, hui e, tāiki e.
Welcome to the gifts of the Earth Mother and Sky Father, bringing us all together.

These are some of the ways we show love and respect when we visit friends and whānau.

Koha kai

Give a gift of food, a little thanks for having us

Moko

Traditional Māori tattoo

You may have seen these moko on Māori. It's good to know the names for the different types, as each has a special meaning.

Mataora
Full-face moko for men

Tīwhana
Moko over the eyebrows

Ngū
Moko on the sides of the nose

Kirituhi
Tattoos that may not be Māori design

Moko kauae
A woman's moko on her chin

Kurawaka
Moko on the forearm
Rape
Moko on the bottom
Puhoro
Moko on the legs

Te arapū Māori
The Māori alphabet

There are five vowels in Māori:

a *('ah')* **e** *('eh')* **i** *('ee')* **o** *('orh')* **u** *('ugh')*

When those letters have a line above them, called a macron, or tohutō, the sound is longer:

ā *('ahhh')* **ē** *('eeeh')* **ī** *('eee')* **ō** *('ooorh')* **ū** *('uuugh')*

A macron makes a word sound quite different and usually changes the meaning of the word, too.

Te arapū Māori also has ten consonants:

h, k, m, n, ng, p, r, t, w, wh

wh *(like 'f' in English)*
ng *(like 'ng' in 'singer')*

Consonants are always combined with a vowel to make a syllable, and that helps us sound out the word. For example, the word 'haka' has two syllables: ha-ka.

To help you even more, you can listen to our pronunciation guide here: